CW01632983

Sam.

Best wishes

Michael

ONCE MORE WITH FEELING

Rehearsal stories from legends and everyday heroes to inspire any performance.

BY
MICHAEL PARKER

First published 2025

All author proceeds go to charity.

Published with assistance from Brown Dog Books
and The Self-Publishing Partnership Ltd.

www.selfpublishingpartnership.co.uk

Printed book ISBN: 978-1-83952-868-2

Designer and editor, Jennifer Kyte.

www.coo-ee.co.uk

Illustration, Cecily Salt

@cecilysalt

This book is printed on FSC® certified paper .

MIX
Paper | Supporting responsible forestry
FSC® C013604
www.fsc.org

oncemorewithfeeling.co.uk

To Julian.

"We are what
we repeatedly do.
Excellence, then, is not
an act, but a habit."

—Aristotle.

CONTENTS

PREFACE

'All the world's a stage and most of us are desperately unrehearsed'.

These words by the Irish poet, Sean O'Casey, are my starting point for this book. There are of course a few, those who make a living through performing, for whom rehearsal is second nature. This holds equally true of artists performing on a stage and of professional athletes in a sport stadium. Jesse Owens, the greatest sprinter of the twentieth century, famously said, *"A lifetime of training for just ten seconds."* For many artists, rehearsal can occupy more of their time than performance.

My own early experience of rehearsal relates only to sport. I was shy as a boy, but highly competitive on the track, enjoying the practice essential to mastering the high hurdler's art. Above everything, I enjoyed racing, the anticipation, the exhilaration of the start. I was then unaware of the concept of mental rehearsal, but I now realise that it enabled me to be my best when it mattered, taking me to two Olympics.

In my advertising career, my competitiveness found an outlet in another race, pitching for business. In a lengthy career, I became less shy and took part in over 1000 pitches. I learnt the hard way, that the more we rehearsed, the more we won. I took this approach into life as a pitch coach, preaching rehearsal. This book develops some of the ideas explored in my first book, *It's Not What You Say, It's The Way You Say It!*, showcasing stories of real people who have benefitted from using rehearsal in their lives.

Various university studies have shown that mental preparation, a vital part of rehearsal, works. Visualising ourselves going through a routine, any routine, improves our chances of success. The same process also helps us solve problems, whatever they are, from frustration, negative thinking to procrastination, one of the commonest barriers to rehearsal!

There are many other barriers, imagined more than real, and most 'rehearsal reluctants' use them. For example, 'I feel too much rehearsal will reduce spontaneity'. Or, 'My content needs more time.' Many do not acknowledge that they are reluctant because they are fearful. The deep-seated fear of public speaking extends to rehearsal, even though rehearsal is the best route to confidence.

Not surprisingly most books on rehearsal are written for stage actors. Much of the content is fascinating but not all is relevant to us non-actors. Characterisation for example. While we are rehearsing to be our best selves, actors are rehearsing to portray someone else.

To encourage the reluctant and fearful, I tell the rehearsal stories of a range of people who perform on very different stages – the classroom, the pulpit, the boardroom, the Zoom call, the TED conference platform, the auction room, the broadcast studio or the sport stadium. Legends or everyday heroes, they share the determination to shine on their chosen stage.

1. HISTORY MAKERS

Few people have spoken so powerfully that they changed history. One of the earliest, notorious for his extreme rehearsal, was Demosthenes. He was not a born orator. He practised and trained like an athlete and worked on his voice. *"His habit to slip pebbles into his mouth and then declaim a number of verses at the top of his voice and without drawing breath, and this not only as he stood still, but while walking about or going up a steep hill."* It was said that when rival orator Cicero finished speaking, the people said, "How well he spoke", but when Demosthenes finished, they said "Let's March!" He convinced fellow Athenians to take up arms against Philip of Macedonia.

Well before the Gettysburg Address, it was Abraham Lincoln's performances 'on the stump' as an orator that created the legend. *"His speech was full of fire and energy and force. It was logic-it was pathos-it was enthusiasm … It was hard-heavy-knotty-gnarly-edged and heated".*

He understood that the way he came across reached hearts. He spent much more time in rehearsal than on the speech, 272 words. He changed American history in less than three minutes.

One of the greatest orators of more recent time was Nelson Mandela. His *ethos*, the appeal of his character, gave added layers of meaning to his brilliant words. Surely, no one was so prepared.

"It is never my custom to use words lightly. If twenty-seven years in prison have done anything to us, it was to use the silence of solitude to make us understand how precious words are and how real speech is in its impact on the way people live and die".

QUEEN ELIZABETH I, NOT SO WEAK AND FEEBLE

"I know I have the body but of a weak and feeble woman; but I have the heart and stomach of a king, and a king of England too"

These words were spoken nearly five hundred years ago by Queen Elizabeth I to her troops, assembled in the early morning mist at Tilbury Docks. They were readying to do battle against the invading Spanish Armada. Her inspirational speech is recognised as one of the greatest in history.

We have first-hand evidence from certain 'noble footmen and great lords' of what she said. We know she was, probably, on horseback, (at any rate, that's how she was portrayed by Cate Blanchett in the movie *Elizabeth*) clad in armour as befitted a warrior monarch. We don't know what she sounded like or even if she could be heard among the jostling soldiers. We do know she motivated and inspired her troops to victory. (Her offer to pay wages due may have played a part).

To understand her remarkable performance, it helps to see her life as one of constant rehearsal, of proving herself as a woman in a world of men, as a monarch deserving of loyalty.

Her early childhood was not easy. When she was two years old, her mother Anne Boleyn was beheaded by her father and she was declared a bastard, unable to inherit the throne. That same father, Henry VIII, did however encourage her education. Extremely intelligent, she studied six languages including Latin and Greek as well as grammar, theology, history, philosophy, mathematics, literature, geometry, logic, and rhetoric. She learnt how to persuade.

Her final tutor, Robert Ascham, pushed her further. He would give her original texts by Demosthenes and Cicero, make her turn them into English, then translate them back into the original language. His aim was that she *"gain purity of style, and from her mind derive instruction that would be of value for her to meet every contingency of life."* At that time, becoming Queen was not an anticipated contingency.

However, when unexpectedly in her twenties she ascended to the throne, she was prepared. Her well-rehearsed skills in oratory allowed her to negotiate with her powerful, all-male Privy Council and to hold sway over

Parliament on the rare occasions she allowed them to sit (only thirteen times in 44 years).

She employed the rhetorical weapons of *pathos*, *logos* and, most tellingly, *ethos*, the appeal of character. Throughout her reign, her well-practised use of *ethos* established her credibility as a leader, able to connect with her people as one of them, despite the attitudes against women at the time.

At Tilbury, she faced the huge challenge of rallying her soldiers. A lifetime of rehearsal enabled her to rise to the occasion. And an understanding of *kairos*, timeliness. Has a speech ever been better suited to the moment of its speaking and the expectation of its audience? No wonder they trusted their "Good Queen Bess."

HITLER AND CHURCHILL, WAR OF WORDS

Two of the greatest orators of the last century were enemies. One wanted to create a Reich to last a thousand years. The other, to lift his people facing defeat. Both held surprisingly similar views on the power of oratory, of the spoken word. In his autobiographical manifesto, *Mein Kampf*, Hitler wrote:

"I know that men are won over less by the written than by the spoken word, that every great movement on this earth owes its growth to great orators and not to great writers."

Churchill, in his novel, *Savrola*, (the central character is a self-portrait) wrote:

"Of all the talents bestowed upon men, none is so precious as the gift of oratory. He who enjoys it wields a power more durable than that of a great king. He is an independent force in the world."

Not surprisingly, both spent years of their lives studying, preparing, and rehearsing oratory to win over their very different audiences. The Germans to suspend all doubt and to follow the Fuhrer; the British to 'never surrender.'

Hitler, unlike Churchill, was a natural orator, initially rousing fervour in the small beer halls of Munich. However, to fulfil his dream of converting mass audiences who would respond to his personal charisma, he would need to perform in huge arenas. This called for a different level of practice and rehearsal.

MEN ARE WON OVER LESS BY THE WRITTEN THAN BY THE SPOKEN WORD.

He studied Wagnerian opera stars, to emulate their command of a stage, and their dramatic gestures. He understood his body language, his naked emotion, and sense of raw power was key to capturing his audience, more than his words. Every facial expression was practiced with the help of a photographer, taking hundreds of thousand shots to identify the strongest, the most compelling gestures, the optimal body movements. He would then rehearse these endlessly to a mirror.

He wrote the speeches himself, often rewriting five times, working through the night. He would practice them out loud, as secretaries edited changes, from the always quiet opening to the screaming crescendo of (apparent or real) rage. He practiced the silences, the pauses, keeping the crowd waiting in suspense. He was, said Goebbels, 'a rhetorical genius of not talking.'

He was a showman, and like today's superstars on tour, his speeches were rehearsed and choreographed to extract maximum response – audiences in their thousands, searchlight displays, dramatic stage entrances, heroic choreography. *"I gradually transformed myself into a speaker for mass meetings [and] I became practiced in the pathos and the gestures which a great hall, with its thousands of people, demands."*

Did this rehearsal pay off? With 5000 speeches in ten years, Hitler turned a party with a mere 3% of the vote into the Government party. In the words of Goebbels,

"He rouses the tired and lazy, fires up the indifferent and the doubting, turns cowards into men and weaklings into heroes."

WE SHALL NEVER SURRENDER.

Winston Churchill was not a natural orator, but he made a lifelong study of rhetoric and the art of public speaking. He read widely, ranging across the ancient Greek classics to Shakespeare, Abraham Lincoln, William Gladstone, and Oliver Cromwell. He often saw his father, leader of the House of Commons and a renowned orator, in action.

Aged just 23 he wrote, but never published, a paper titled *The Scaffolding of Rhetoric.* It's five principles still hold good.

In summary:

Correct diction. *"Use the best possible word . . . short, homely words . . . so long as such words can fully express the speaker's thoughts and feelings."*

Rhythm. *"Create a rhythmic flow of sounds with long, rolling, sonorous sentences and balanced phrases."*

Accumulation of argument. *"Leading the audience convincingly to the climax by a rapid succession of waves of sound and vivid pictures."*

Analogy. *"Apt analogies are among the most formidable weapons of the rhetorician."*

Extravagance of language. *"Some expression must be found that will represent all they are feeling."*

Putting these principles into practice was a challenge for Churchill. He suffered speech impediments of both a stammer and a lisp. A throat specialist advised that only practice and perseverance would help. He practised diligently, rehearsing aloud *"The Spanish ships I cannot see since they are not in sight"* to stop stumbling over words starting with 's'. He spoke as often as possible, and even though the lisp persisted, he overcame his nervousness and inhibition.

He wrote all his own speeches, some 3000 of them in 55 years. Typically, he would do several handwritten drafts, before having them typed up in a manner that helped delivery, with breaks in sentences to indicate the deliberate pauses, or the changes in tempo and emphasis.

He rehearsed aloud, often in front of a mirror, practising every aspect of delivery, from tone and pace to body language and expression. As he practiced, he was always seeking ways to project his unique personality, his character and sense of purpose to best engage with his audience. In his words:

"His ideas began to take the form of words, to group themselves into sentences; he murmured to himself, the rhythm of his own language swayed him; instinctively he alliterated. . . That was a point; could not tautology accentuate it? The sound would please their ears, the sense improve and stimulate their minds."

Did his rehearsal pay off? He was awarded a Nobel Prize for his writings and brilliant oratory. We did not surrender.

History, as the film *The King's Speech* reminds us, also tells the story of King George VI in this war of words. From birth he had suffered from a stammer causing extreme anxiety when speaking. He rehearsed, for one hour every day with his speech therapist, working on pausing and swapping words for something easier to pronounce. His iconic radio broadcast on September 3rd, 1939, opened with these words,

"In this grave hour, perhaps the most fateful in our history, for the second time in the lives of most of us, we are at war."

He did not stutter.

RONALD REGAN, THE GREAT COMMUNICATOR

Ronald Regan, a Republican, was the 40th president of the United States. When he took office in 1981, he was the oldest to be elected, serving two terms until 1989. Today, most non-Americans will remember him as a onetime Hollywood actor who, like Arnold Schwarzenegger many years later, went on to be Governor of California. Unlike Arnie, who was disqualified having been born outside USA, Regan went on to become President.

Old news clips capture his genial smiling face when in conversation with close ally, Margaret Thatcher, as well as with rival Mikhail Gorbachev, the man with whom he paved the way to better relations with the USSR. In America, together with Abraham Lincoln and Barack Obama, he is considered one the greatest presidential orators. He was known as 'the Great Communicator.'

His life can be seen as one of constant rehearsal, readying him for his biggest performance role, that of President. His first job was on a local radio station where he learnt *"to talk to your audience, not over their heads or through them. Don't try to talk in a special language of broadcasting or even of politics, just use normal everyday words."* As an unscripted sport commentator, talking under pressure and off-the-cuff became second nature, something that would serve him well in his political life.

His success as a radio performer led to the call from Hollywood. There he became an actor. A good one who honed his craft, rehearsing and starring in some seventy films. Playing a part became natural and, in all but one of his films, he played the 'good guy', not the villain. The down to earth, humorous optimist persona, key to his political success, was consolidated. As a captain during the war, he served in a wartime motion picture unit producing some 400 training films. He understood performance from both sides of the camera.

Having mastered radio and film, he moved into television, then increasingly taking its place as the medium of influence. In the fifties, he hosted one of the top-rated network programmes, showcasing 235 plays over six years. This gave him invaluable experience of live broadcast. (Trump, fifty years later, was to benefit from his experience hosting the American version of *The Apprentice*.) A spin-off from the television show was an annual countrywide tour delivering speeches to workforces, sometimes as many as fourteen a day! With that level of practice, no wonder he made political speeches seem effortless.

Arguably no one entered political life so comfortable in rehearsal, so confident in what worked for him. He instructed his script writers to stick to his template for a good speech – they were to be no longer than twenty minutes (TED Talks are 18 minutes) and follow the (classic) format *"tell them what you're going to tell them, tell them, and then tell them what you've told them."* He felt deeply that a speech must consider the audiences' mood and guide their passions and emotions, while using the words of the common man. It was vital 'to be honest in what you're saying' and 'to be in touch with your audience.'

Carefully crafted scripts were subjected to rigorous rehearsal, where Regan would add stories and humorous anecdotes, putting his personal stamp on the speech. His 'honeyed' voice worked equally well in a fireside chat broadcast as in a major platform speech. He could 'keep your attention reading from the phone book', but his use of language, the timing, the easy delivery, and injections of humour made his performances compelling. One of his earlier speeches, *A Time for Choosing*, is widely regarded as among the greatest of the twentieth century.

Regan was a master of persuasive speaking, but it was his manner, his personality that so lifted his performances. A politician, he came across as non-political, an honest straight talking, 'one of us.' Reagan himself credited his political success to an empathy with ordinary Americans. To one reporter, who asked what people saw in him, Reagan replied: *"Would you laugh if I told you that I think, maybe, they see themselves, and that I'm one of them? I've never been able to detach myself or think that I, somehow, am apart from them."*

One story captures the essence of his performing genius. In a presidential debate with his much younger rival Walter Mondale, he faced tough questions. Was he getting too old for the job? Did he worry he might not have the necessary energy? With a gentle smile, and perfect comedic timing (undoubtedly rehearsed) he replied:

"No, I don't, and I will not make age an issue of this campaign. I am not going to exploit, for political purposes, my opponent's youth and inexperience."

The audience, including Walter Mondale, burst into laughter. It was recognised as a defining moment leading to his eventual victory.

FOOTNOTE

Whether you are making history or simply want to get a point across, there is nothing as powerful as the spoken word. Oratory. Hitler knew this so did Churchill. To do it well, to persuade people to your point of view, you must harness the three appeals of *ethos*, your character, *logos*, reason, and *pathos*, emotion. Great speakers rehearse relentlessly to master these.

As Quintilian said two thousand years ago,

"I would not hesitate to assert that a mediocre speech supported by all the power of delivery will be more impressive than the best speech unaccompanied by such power."

2. BUSINESS LEADERS

There are many styles of leadership from democratic to autocratic, from laissez-faire to visionary, but all call for a high level of communication performance. Whether you are an extrovert or an introvert, your performance is always under scrutiny by your teams, on the factory floor, in an open plan office or the board room. Or on Zoom. You are 'on show.' They look to you to lead by example, to set the mood, optimistic, confident, or defiant and resolute. What you say matters, but the way you say it matters so much more.

Leaders understand this and recognise that, while some delegation is possible, they must themselves master communication skills. They may do this through classic preparation and rehearsal, preferably to an objective outsider who can tell them how they come across to their audience. Are they talking with them not at them, sharing not proclaiming, empathetic. They may also, as many do, rehearse 'in the mind,' assessing options and possible courses of action. Being prepared. In sport this is sometimes referred to as the 'inner game.'

Steve Jobs broke the mould with his approach to perfecting performance in the business world. He recognised its remarkable power to influence behaviour. He saw how that power could be magnified if exercised in person by the leader of the company. Not naturally gifted, he gave himself the challenge, through rehearsal, of becoming the shining star of his show.

Orson Welles channelled his genius as a writer, director, and actor to produce, and star in Citizen Kane, one of the greatest movies of all time. Jobs, seemingly, set out to make each of his legendary presentations his next Citizen Kane. He applied intensively all the rehearsal and practices that are part and parcel of the professional stage actor getting into a role. For him this was the role of 'visionary leader'. During rehearsal, he would step out of this role as he paused to ask his team for critique.

A common excuse by many who avoid it, is the belief that too much rehearsal inhibits spontaneity. Jobs did not hold this view. He rehearsed to enable spontaneity. *"I mean his whole thing of knowing exactly what he's going to say, but up on stage saying it in such a way that makes you think he's thinking it up right then …"* — Bill Gates.

Another observer said, *"This was one of Steve's great secrets as a presenter. He practiced. A lot. He went over and over until he had the presentation honed and he knew it cold."* He methodically internalised the material on every slide, he thought about what each line meant to him and what this line meant to an audience. He worked on pace, on using his voice and his gestures to supplement his words.

If Steve Jobs drew mainly from the acting world for his rehearsal approach, others draw from competitive sport, a much-used metaphor for corporate strategy. The combination of oratory and athletic practice and rehearsal is not new. In Ancient Greece athletic instruction was used to create rhetorical training based on rhythm, repetition, and response.

Jobs could have been a formidable athlete!

A CORPORATE CEO

Before joining global real estate company CBRE, where he is now a leader, Ciaran Bird played rugby for London Irish. He was coached by Clive Woodward, who later coached England, where his approach to performance analysis and rehearsal are legendary. Ciaran talked enthusiastically about the astonishing level of rehearsal that Woodward went through preparing England for the 2003 World Cup final, the last one they won!

> "He and the team would have analysed it way before the match itself. Every potential situation you could have had, everything at every minute and every time. What if this happened? What if they score? What if someone gets sent off? What if this? What if it's extra time? And there's a drop goal? What is it we're gonna do? They rehearsed all that many times before, and they knew!"

Ciaran took the lessons learnt chasing success in the intensely competitive world of professional rugby into his business life.

"Do you know whether I listen to you, whether it's a commentator, whether it's a manager or coach, whether it's a player, whether it's an actor the very, very best of them work harder than anybody else. Take Ronaldo, you could say he's just a born genius. And you could say does he really need to work that hard. He trains harder than anybody. Spends more time practicing than anybody."

Ciaran has focused on creating a great sense of teamwork right across the company, introducing the 'teamship' rules set out in Woodward's book, *Winning*.

"It's the same with introducing new best practices in our people, our teams. We keep on and on practicing them. We 'reboot them' every year otherwise people fall back into old, complacent ways. We work harder, more worried about it than anyone else."

Ciaran claims he is not a natural performer, so he doesn't spare himself when it comes to rehearsal, leaving little to chance. However, whether he is preparing for a large-scale stage presentation with audio visual backup, or a more informal management gathering, he makes sure any rehearsal releases spontaneity rather than stifle it. Authenticity is everything.

"I believe, whilst I wouldn't use the right words and the right emphasis all the time, the way that you would, the audience knows I'm real, and it's me. And my audience at work, they know me. They know if I read something, and it wasn't mine, they'd know a mile off, right? And so, I try and get real with it, and I probably do make mistakes, but I think they forgive me, because they know it's the passion of me ... and the real me."

Naturally highly competitive, Ciaran sees rehearsal as a natural part of business success ...

"Whether it's rehearsing, whether it's 'capturing', whether it's learning from your mistakes and your successes. It's absolutely driven into me. Rehearsal is about being the best you can be."

A CULTURAL CEO

The London Philharmonic Orchestra has been celebrated as one of the world's great orchestras since Sir Thomas Beecham founded it in 1932. Its home is at the Southbank Centre's Royal Festival Hall. It was heralded in The Times as *"London's most dynamic mainstream orchestra."*

Whilst musical, David Burke is not one of the orchestra's musicians, he is the dynamic CEO. In this role, the stage on which he performs regularly is the imposing board room. He prepares well in advance, deciding not just what he needs to say but how he wants to come across, how he will 'own' the room. One way is to own the seating plan. The formidable Angela Merkel, when chancellor of Germany, would rearrange the chairs at a conference herself to better command the room.

He makes use of the 'rule of three', a way of structuring an argument that makes it easy to deliver, and easy for his colleagues to take in. To change pace, to grab attention, he practises the all-important … pause. Something the musician board members appreciate. After all, it was Claude Debussy who said, *"Music is the space between the notes."*

In carrying out beforehand this mental rehearsal of his own performance, familiarising himself with its content, David frees himself of worry about how he is coming across when he takes the stage. The worry that undermines confident performance. He's free to care about 'them', to channel energy outwards to his audience of fellow board members.

"What's in it for them?" The question any speaker must have in mind. How can he bring them into the meeting as active players, not passive observers? He spends time and thought, visualising, *"how to bring other people on stage. I set out to create a space where ideas spread,"*

David takes rehearsal seriously. So too, of course, does the principal conductor of the orchestra, Edward Gardener, who says:

"He is more nervous before the first rehearsal of the orchestra than he is before the first performance!"

THE START-UP

You have a brilliant innovative idea for a new service. You have perfected and rehearsed the argument. All that remains is the pitch to investors. A make-or-break opportunity.

This is the moment of truth behind the globally successful television show *Dragon's Den*. First created in Japan, it captures the drama and the suspense of the start-up pitch. The potential investors, like Caesar ready with their thumbs to award the successful untold riches, dooming the failures to the waiting lions. The baying crowds, the viewers, revel in the suspense, the agony, the ecstasy.

Most of the gladiators have genuinely original ideas, eye-catching if not practical and (fairly) well-rehearsed pitches. The dragons are quick to spot the errors in the arguments. Memorable storytelling stands out. One of the best was Levi Roots, playing his guitar while telling the story of his grandmother's secret recipe for his *Reggae Reggae* sauce. It went on to become a global brand.

Olga Turner did not have to worry about the TV viewers when she launched her company Ekkist with the compelling concept, "the UK's first healthy building consultancy."

She was not fighting for her life, but she was fighting for her fledgling company and the health of others. She drew on World Health Organisation data, fascinating building experiments, and technology to support her concept. To make it tangible, she told stories from countries where healthy buildings were already a dramatic signal of the future. *"In Milan the remarkable Bosch Verticale (vertical forest), in the form of two biophilically designed skyscrapers, houses as many trees as could be planted in nearly two acres of forest."*

Her forensically prepared argument and a well-rehearsed, emotionally powerful delivery struck a chord with investors and early adopter clients. Ekkist is now an established leader in its field.

The learning Olga takes from this intense rehearsal experience includes the pitfall of being, or appearing to be, over rehearsed. Too much time and effort spent learning your script by heart, and perfecting the use of visual aids, can lead to a 'mechanical' performance. The lack of spontaneity creates a distance from the audience, a feeling you are not in touch with them.

This awareness of her audience, her empathy, is significant. She 'cares' for her audience, rather than worry about herself. Before any meeting, she 'rehearses in her mind' the right way to connect with each audience. Are they looking for a friendly chat, a formal approach, lots of hard facts, or passion? Reading the audience and not being caught up in your own performance is key.

CARE FOR YOUR AUDIENCE.

This is not made easier by Zoom where reading the room, and the body language is almost impossible. The sense of theatre that comes with the live pitch or presentation is also lacking. The Zoom meeting is too easy to cancel, the audience has a lower sense of anticipation. Important presentation meetings are less special, which makes finding the right balance of emotion and reason that much harder.

Olga's final learning is perhaps the most important. However brilliant the argument, she believes start-ups will be judged on the personality of the entrepreneur. This puts authenticity at the heart of success.

"Rehearsal that encourages spontaneity, rather than a rigid script delivery, allows the real you to shine".

The real Olga was elected to Forbes 30 Under 30 Hall of Fame.

"The mother of art is architecture. Without an architecture of our own we have no soul of our own civilization."

— Frank Lloyd Wright.

THE ARCHITECT

Architects have a lot to live up to. What may have started out as a rough pencil sketch could end up, many months later, as a finished design, in model and graphic form, a submission for a new Nature and Wellbeing centre. One of several entrants to be presented to a panel of judges. The winner becoming a building that will have soul.

The model will be so complete that judges can 'walk though' every room, in virtual reality. Where does this leave a role for the mere human architect presenter. What needs to be said?

Architect Duncan McLeod feels that only some 20% of the presentation will rest on the physical, the rational elements of the design. The judges need much more than this from their architect to persuade them in their decision making. They need his belief, his story, and his passion. They need to share his feeling for what is in front of them. After all, they will need to share and pass on this feeling to everyone who will be touched by the building they are investing in.

For Duncan, expressing these feelings in the best possible way is the product of considerable rehearsal. He has found his starting point for a presentation is often that of finding the story. A story grounded in truth and belief. A story that can be naturally told and which will resonate with his audience.

Through rehearsal, he has learnt that the more conversational his approach, the more relaxed and receptive his audience will be. Without rehearsal, he finds a lack of preparation can lead to his old lecturing, reading from a script style. If the presentation is all about transmitting information and not about conversing, he becomes a different person. Not his normally nice self.

In conveying his feelings, his enthusiasm, he misses when zooming, the classic sketching, during the meeting, to explain and engage. To minimise this loss of 'human' connection, he has found rehearsing with all the technical and digital wizardry available – endless white boards, split screens, digitally generated diagrams – ensures that engaging conversation, not the 'brilliant' visuals, carry the persuasion. The way he says it will always evoke more feeling than any AI augmented aid.

Since he feels that some 80% of the pitch effect is down to the intangibles, the feelings experienced and passions shared, he has developed his own routine of 'rehearsing in the mind.' This started with him coming to terms with fear, the fear of public speaking common to most of us. He works hard on his mental approach, captured as "a fear is only a thought, it's not real."

A FEAR IS ONLY A THOUGHT, IT'S NOT REAL.

He rehearses in his mind to clear the baggage of worrying about how he comes across. He visualises and "pictures the presentation setting," to have a wider view, being able to assess the feelings of his audience, and their concerns. Are they introvert or extrovert, are they task driven, or people based? However brilliant his design, unless he reaches them on an emotional level he'll fail. He will often check-in at the end of a meeting and say, "was that helpful?" or "are you happy?"

Remote audiences are less easily read. "*Your body language is diminished, making it harder for each of you to pick up the subtleties of communication.*" Duncan treats this as a challenge, and practices to make Zoom 'empathetic.' Replicating the normal behaviour of informal live meetings, putting everyone at ease, establishing rapport, not allowing the impersonal 'click to join' to dictate proceedings. His conversational approach comes into its own.

"*For me rehearsal all comes back to you creating a conversation, so they don't feel they are being peppered with information. It allows a trust to develop.*" Duncan takes to heart the words of Truman Capote, "*A conversation is a dialogue not a monologue.*"

TWO AUCTIONEERS

Read this aloud, as fast as you can.

"I have one pound, I have one, give me two, give me two, I have two, give me three, give me three, give me three, I have three, give me four, give me four, I have four, give me five, give me five, I have five, give me six, give me six..."

This is the basis of the bidding call or auction chant. It has three components. The price of the last bid. The bid to come and 'filler' words ('give me' ... 'I have,' words that help the rhythm of the call and offer thinking time, very little, for the bidders.)

The oldest auctioneer school in the world is in the USA. The Mississippi School, the 'Harvard of Auctioneering,' has an online video of a class in action. It shows a mesmerising scene of some 60 students, chanting in unison. It also shows individuals practising the chant and their facial expression.

Each student has the goal of finding a call unique to them, in style, rhythm, and cadence. A call that energises onlookers, draws them in to what is a 'conversation' with the auctioneer, the silent language of the twitch of an eyebrow, brief nod, touching an ear, raising the programme, or a studied disinterest. It is a language the auctioneer must listen to, and interpret instantly, as he chants, responding without breaking his rhythm. This takes a lot of practice.

While chanting is critical to what is, in effect, a form of performance art, the auctioneer needs much more. He or she must bring the confidence of a stand-up comedian (and the timing), the persuasiveness of a top salesperson and the knowledge of a specialist in the chosen field. From house clearance to houses, cattle to cars, charity to world famous art. Introducing the next lot of unruly bullocks to a crowd of seasoned farmers is not the same as extolling the genius behind a piece of artwork. Bidders will only feel comfortable if reassured by the auctioneer's ability to talk their language, whether that's 'cow' or 'art.'

Stories of two very different individuals, both formidably practised, both knowing how to rehearse to perform at their best, demonstrate the art in practice.

A leading auctioneer in the USA, where they do things bigger and sell them faster, is T.F.Freije, 'the man with the golden tongue.' A former International (i.e. USA) National champion, at his most rapid, he can sell more than 100 lots an hour. An article by David Gendelman tells "how he takes a deep breath and launches into the vocal equivalent of a virtuoso banjo solo, tongue picking syllables with unrelenting cadence." The keys to a good bid chant, says Freije, are speed, clarity, and rhythm. "Really enunciating and opening your mouth and popping your lips."

An in-house interview with a very different personality, John Hays, one of Christie's leading art auctioneers, tells a story where the chant may have a different cadence, but principles don't change. His style reflects his audience. For a major artwork worth many millions, there may be as few as six serious bidders.

"For an hour and a half, John masterfully guides the vibe of the saleroom. His gestures command attention. His moments of silence hold the room in suspense. His shooting eye contact singles out the newest bidder. But just as easily, he can flip the energy, joking with the audience and addressing phone operators by name. Then when the moment feels right, a swift pound of the gavel rips through the space..."

Hays says:

> "You're in a theatre. You have to be able to keep people interested. You have to keep people amused. You have to be serious in your purpose. The art of auctioneering is probably the least understood and maybe perhaps, after the art itself, is the most important factor in what happens at Christie's."

A good auctioneer can add 20% to the bid price. Going once. Going twice...

GOING ONCE!

GOING TWICE!!

A MILITARY STRATEGIST

The Art of War is a favourite among armchair business warriors. It's all there. Campaign strategies, guerrilla tactics, war games, leadership contests, gaining footholds and winning pitch battles.

Written around 500 BCE by Sun Tzu, it makes no reference to rehearsal. The word only appeared over a thousand years later, from the Old French, *remercier*, raking over old ground (some rehearsals can seem like that), repeating, reiterating, saying over again.

What Sun Tzu does do is talk about preparation.

"To ... not prepare is the greatest of crimes; to be prepared beforehand for any contingency is the greatest of virtues." And *"He will win who, prepared himself, waits to take the enemy unprepared."*

Nor does he talk specifically about mental rehearsal. But he understood its essence.

"When you know both yourself as well as your competition, you are never in danger. To know yourself and not others, gives you half a chance of winning. Knowing neither yourself nor your competition puts you in a position to lose."

BUSINESS BRIEF

These stories tell us how different leaders have won over critically important audiences. They have prepared the best possible arguments. They have rehearsed their own performance. They have put themselves in the shoes of their audience to anticipate how they might think or feel.

In any workplace, in any task from customer facing to back-room operation, you will be communicating, negotiating, persuading, placating, on a daily basis. You may be good at this, or think you are. You could be better. Rehearsal will help, from pausing to think before you speak, taking time to prepare your message, reminding yourself to listen, to show empathy.

"Far from making you appear robotic or canned, rehearsal frees you to enjoy the moment and deliver your message with passion and energy."

— Carmine Gallo

3. STAGE PERFORMERS

I can find no mention of the earliest rehearsal but there are records from cave paintings 20,000 years ago of men dancing. I suspect they rehearsed their dance moves alongside spear hurling practice. Theatre as an art form has flourished since around 500 BC and so too has rehearsal.

Performance artists – actors, dancers, musicians – unlike most of us, are rehearsing with others, interpreting a score, a character, a role, while fulfilling the demands of a director or conductor. They are always learning, living in rehearsal for much of their lives. They have all found ways of being at their best when the curtain goes up. We can learn from them.

THE VIOLIN SOLOIST

From a solid base of her conventional classical education, Esther Abrami has carved out an international career that defies convention. A vision, underpinned by the rigorous discipline of practice and rehearsal, has led violinist Esther to a far from conventional success on a global stage.

She decided she wanted to be a violinist when she was ten years old. After her early years of study in France she went to Cheetham's School of Music in Manchester and then to the Royal College of Music in London. At both, she underwent the challenging regimes of study, practice and rehearsal, and the examinations essential to any aspiring musician. She said that she found time spent practicing for exams "took away the whole joy of sharing her music. Then at the few concerts I did play, there was a very specific type of audience that wasn't very diverse."

This observation helped form her vision, a vision that was to bring classical music to a wider younger audience in an accessible manner, not constrained by the staid, stuffy approach of much of the industry. She talked to her young social media audience in their language, in their medium, in her own authentic voice. She was the first classical musician to be nominated in the Social Media Superstar category at the Global awards.

Among her numerous and engaging posts on TikTok and Instagram, she revealed insights into her daily practice and rehearsal routines. Posts would show her in the early stages of learning new pieces, snippets of practice sessions, comparing different violins, doing shifting exercises, rehearsal with an orchestra, getting ready to go on stage. Her followers could see the highs and the lows of preparation, get a sense of what it takes, emotionally and physically to reach the top. These fascinating glimpses of Esther in rehearsal could only hint at the discipline and the hours spent each day.

For Esther the goal is performance. To bring her best self to her playing and to delight her audiences with her music. Her success in living her vision has already, early in her career, led to performances in cities and concert venues around the world, including the legendary Albert Hall. I asked her three questions about how she prepared to 'be her best self', when it really matters, performing for audiences in the thousands.

As a violin soloist, unlike the orchestra, you can't have the music in front of you as you play. How do you play with such confidence?

ESTHER: *"Really there were several things. Firstly, I made sure that I knew the piece so well that I could wake up in the middle of the night and play it, that I knew it inside out. It's a beautiful orchestral piece so I worked on the orchestra scores so there was a lot of practice which was outside, away from my violin and just with the score and learning the whole score by memory. I think a lot of people underestimate musicians and the practice that we can do away from the instrument, and memorising you can do just as well, nearly better away from the instrument."*

"Obviously when you have the pressure of a concert, memory is so important. Memory slip is one of the of the fears of musicians, to forget what you're going to play, so knowing really deep the absolute every corner of the score so that if anything happens you can catch yourself and come back to it and do it so nobody will even realize that you've had a slight moment of, you know, hesitation or something."

How does your rehearsal for a performance differ from your normal routine?

ESTHER: *"It's a sort of mental process I guess, absolutely. There is the physical process of course, which is the kind of eight hours a day practice, but there's also a huge mental practice, especially when we talk about performance, when we talk for example about the Royal Albert Hall. We have a huge hall with a very big audience so what I did for that I worked a lot on picturing how it was going to be."*

PICTURE HOW IT'S GOING TO BE.

"I did a lot of visualization. I did 'fake' performances asking some people to sit in, as if I was in the concert situation and then actually picturing the Albert Hall in my head and visualizing that, and playing with feeling so I can feel a little bit the pressure that I would get on stage. When you do that, you can imagine the hall filled with people."

"Also, I record myself to add a pressure. It's basically pushing yourself as close as you can do into the situation that you will be in on the day, that way it allows me to be much less nervous because I feel like it's something I've nearly done before even though obviously it's not, but you've had experience this close to that and it feels like you're prepared mentally. It's a whole process of imagining the idea, of accepting this idea and getting used to this idea so that you're not scared on the day."

> What do you feel makes someone a great performer?

ESTHER: *"It's not something you're born with. There's a huge learning curve of understanding that it's not because you practice all those hours in your practice room, in your bedroom, the physical kind of repeating making sure you know the part. Nothing will replace experience, and nothing will replace the proactive thing to be on a stage, practicing feeling the pressure, there is nothing that can replace that. If you suddenly start performing and shake with nerves, you've not done the 'bridge' of going from pure practice, rehearsing something bit by bit, and never doing a run through fully of the piece. You have always got to practice the way you're going to perform with that idea in mind."*

THE ACTOR

For professional actors, rehearsal is integral to their craft as they prepare to deliver scripts not written by them, meet the demands of a director and entertain their audiences. Unlike 'non-acting' performers, they are rehearsing to play a role, to bring alive a character. Most of us rehearse to be ourselves, our best selves!

Imogen Sage is an actor who has performed on stages as different, and far apart, as Shakespeare's Globe Theatre in London and Sydney's iconic Opera House. She first lent me her expertise for my book on presentation, *It's Not What You Say, It's The Way You Say it!* To provide some insight to the difference in approach, I talked to her about rehearsing, handling the demands of a script, making a role her own and connecting with the audience.

"Every actor has their own way of working. After time you find what works for you. My approach to rehearsal changes for every job I do, and this is because every job is different. I work very instinctively in rehearsals, constantly asking questions. What do I need to research? Why does my character do this? Why do they say that? How do they move? How do they think? What do I want to bring to this performance?"

"For me, there are two types of preparation: the preparation that happens in the lead up to, and over the rehearsal period, and the preparation that happens in the hours before the show begins."

"During the rehearsal period my own private preparation work includes a lot of research and daydreaming, reading the script quietly to myself over and over again so that I become familiar with it, and finding physicality."

"I often break my script up into sections, or units, based on when my character changes tactic in a scene. At the beginning of each unit, I write my intention, for example: to convince, to charm, to seduce, to make someone understand me, to inspire, to excite, to calm, to reassure etc. This helps me focus on smaller chunks of the script so that I can find a more detailed, less generalised performance."

"When I start to learn my lines, I tend to move around a lot, or go for a walk to get the lines in my body. Sometimes I stomp around the room, or dance, or even just do the dishes. All of this helps me embody the words. It helps me get energy moving and get out of my head."

"I also try to find a need to speak – when we speak, we have something we need to communicate, or else why talk at all? So, I try to connect with what that need is for my character, and where it sits in my body. It might be something like "I need to win his trust" or "I need to convince him to stay" or "I need to inspire him to consider a different way", or "I need to make him laugh". And this might sit in my gut, or in my heart, or somewhere else. When you're acting from need, what happens is always fresh. No-one wants to watch something that seems pre-prepared. They want to see spontaneity and aliveness on stage."

REHEARSAL IS WHERE THE MAGIC HAPPENS.

“For me, rehearsals are where the magic happens. It’s the time and space to explore, develop, and take risks.”

“Theatre actors spend weeks exploring different creative options and making offers. The director and cast work together to discover the blocking – where to stand, when to enter and exit, and when and how to move. But the actors also use the rehearsal period to find the physicality and the inner life of their characters, their motivations and emotional core.”

“This takes time. It’s not something that can happen in front of an audience easily, when nerves are present, or when there are other technical markers to hit. When an actor is performing in front of an audience, they are following a blueprint they’ve already lined out. It may not be exactly the same performance every night. In fact, hopefully it’s different. But the actor is following an outline they have already discovered in rehearsals.”

“Rehearsals are also about bonding with your cast, working together as a team and hopefully having a good time! The show is always better if the actors are working together and supporting each other. I think the audience can feel it too.”

“Pre-performance, before I go on stage, I warm-up. This includes relaxation, stretching, warming up my voice, going through my lines one last time, and connecting with my cast mates. Saying hi to them. Asking them about their day. It's good to get the attention off yourself. A performance is always more engaging when we're not self-conscious. All the work should be done by now. In the 30 minutes before the show, it's time to connect with the cast, tune in with the audience, and ride the wave."

Imogen is talking as an actor, but her main observations hold true for any performer. People want to feel that you are saying what you are saying to them, and only them, for the first time.

"The most engaging are those who are focusing on who they are speaking to, not on themselves. The more you rehearse, the more you can be free in performance."

THE CHOIR

Long before Gareth Malone and his Army Wives appeared to acclaim on BBC television, choir singing was well-established in the UK. At the last count, some 40,000 choirs are active with well over two million people singing on a regular basis — choral societies, rock choirs, church and, of course, community choirs. That is more than the number who play football, the country's favourite sport.

The small town of Wincanton boasts such a community choir. A recent advertisement, attracting new members, set out to allay common nervousness while capturing the benefits and enjoyment of singing along:

Singing? Who? Me?

> "Most choirs are made up of people who sang at school. Some are sight-readers. Some are not. The rewards are huge. Not only is singing good for your physical health – it is a genuine work out – but you are also taxing your brain and memory. And on top of that, together with the other singers around you, you become part of a bigger collective sound. That is very fulfilling."

Administratively, the choir runs itself, but the fulcrum, the inspiration for the singing, is the Musical Director. For Wincanton, this was Katrine Reimers. She has a formidable track record that extends from rehearsing school children, sometimes nine sessions of 30 pupils in a single day, to a massed choir of 3,000 in Italy. In a typical week, she will rehearse five evenings of different community choirs like Wincanton (Mondays at 7.15!) Rehearsal is her life.

The choir members know better than to arrive late. If they do, they miss the essential warm-up I asked Katrine to explain its importance:

"With amateur choirs, you work on the basis they have not come in having prepared their voices, so that very moment doesn't feel ready to start singing. To begin the session, I just need focus and I need silence."

"The first ten minutes or so is just working on posture, breathing, and extending right through the range of voice you've got to use, concentrating on watching, and so much of that is listening to what they're doing, hearing what's not working that day and what needs to be improved and worked on. It's the first moment of focus, doing something together that has to be timed together. Collectively doing something together at the same time is an essential but taken for granted. Without it, you have a totally dysfunctional choir."

"An essential start, a warm-up is really, really, important, encouraging people to think about how they are breathing, and listening to the sound they are making when they are not under the stress of trying to sing the right notes – at the right time with complicated music — and all that, pulling out the thread. This is your physical activity, and this is how to have your body ready. Hopefully, they can reconnect with that as rehearsal continues. Every warm-up is different because I hear different things. It takes years to internalise these things and really get the hang of them."

And that's just the warm-up!

I watch from the pews as the rehearsal proper gets under way. Katrine goes into a remarkable 90-minute podium performance of sustained energy, energy that fuels the choir. One moment she conducts the whole choir, the next the tenors. She explains what she wants from the altos, she answers questions, demonstrates by singing.

She conducts with exaggerated movement to emphasise and exhort, avoiding monologue but using active conversation.

She paces the rehearsal to balance singing (which all enjoy) with necessary practice, and throughout listening and hearing the choir, all the time hoping for moments of real focus, a collective moment when you hear it in the breathing. These moments don't always arrive but aiming for them is her goal.

HAIL!
BRIGHT
CECILIA.

While rehearsal is the enjoyable weekly cake, the icing is the public concert. For the Wincanton choir, this was *'A Delightfully English Concert'* of music in St Luke's Church. For Katrine, the dress rehearsal the afternoon before was the most demanding. For the first and only time, she has brought the choir, the orchestra, and the soloists together. The warm-up, capturing focus, was at its most important. The rehearsal paid off. A packed church, for the single performance, enjoyed Henry Purcell's famous ode, written over three hundred years ago, *Hail! Bright Cecilia.*

St Cecilia, patron saint of musicians, is reported to have said, *"It was heavenly."*

THE WITNESS

"I knew Bill Cosby was going to try to ruin me." In my search for unexpected stories of rehearsal, I came across this remarkable story in a Guardian interview. It describes the way one of his victims prepared to give her crucial evidence in his trial.

The key witness was Andrea Constand, a former professional basketball player.

She prepared for her cross-examination in the way she had always trained, with constant repetition to master a skill, going over her account and practising her responses to the point of exhaustion. She even used the same visualisation that helped her before big matches – except instead of picturing herself scoring, she was in the stand, looking the defence attorney in the eye. "It wasn't a 'competition'," says Constand, "but it was a legal marathon."

THE COMEDIAN (FORMER DOCTOR)

These are words from a *Desert Island Discs* interview with doctor turned author and comedian, Adam Kay.

> "So, tell me about the adrenaline rush of performing live. Because you have had many sold out shows and tours. Is there a comparison to the adrenaline rush similar to appearing in theatre? Obviously, lives are not at stake."

ADAM: *"Being a doctor, totally ruins your barometer for things that you get scared or excited about. I never get excited or scared about going on stage because what's the worst that could happen? Everyone asks for a refund or throws things at me for an hour. That's what people say at work, but in my old job they would die, and it would be my fault if they did."*

AN ICON

I am not a 'Swiftie,' but, like much of the world, I can't help but be impressed.

Impressed that ten American college classes are devoted to Taylor Swift, including Harvard where the professor likens her work to William Wordsworth. Impressed that her 2023/24 *Eras Tour* pulled in over two billion dollars. Impressed that world leaders like Canada's prime minister are asking her to tour in their country. Impressed that her show lasts over 180 minutes, including 40-plus songs, with over 16 costume changes.

"I knew this tour was harder than anything I'd ever done before by a long shot."

And it's no surprise that I'm impressed by her approach to rehearsal. When she was made Time magazine's Person of the Year 2023, she reveals, in the accompanying article, insights into her intense routine.

She began training six months ahead of the first show. "Every day I would run on the treadmill, singing the entire set list out loud," she said. "Fast for fast songs, and a jog or a fast walk for slow songs." Her gym created a program for her, incorporating strength, conditioning, and weights. "Then I had three months of dance training, because I wanted to get it in my bones," she says.

"I wanted to be so over-rehearsed that I could be silly with the fans, and not lose my train of thought."

Maintaining her strength through workouts is key. "I know I'm going on that stage whether I'm sick, injured, heartbroken, uncomfortable or stressed," she says. "That's part of my identity as a human being now. If someone buys a ticket to my show, I'm going to play it unless we have some sort of force majeure."

Singing forty songs, while pounding a treadmill, is taking physical and mental rehearsal to a new level. Akin to Demosthenes with pebbles in his mouth, walking up hill, declaiming verses at the top of his voice. Keeping her fans in mind as she rehearses is a lesson for all of us who, caught up in our own rehearsal, worry more about ourselves, than about our intended audience.

While the practice and rehearsal for *Era*'s exceeds anything Swift has done before, serious preparation has long been her focus. Over ten years ago, while writing my book, *The Wedding Speech Made Easy*, I came across, and happily used, her great quote:

"I try to prepare for everything beyond the extent of preparation."

UPSTAGED

A few years ago, in a session at a literary festival, I was one of thirty writers allowed two minutes to 'sell' our latest book to the audience. Most of us had prepared well and earned polite applause. The last speaker, frail and elderly, spoke haltingly to rapturous response.

I later discovered he had been a professional actor all his life. Unlike me and my fellow writers focussed on the merits of our work, he cared for the audience, and what was in it for them. They not only applauded, but they also bought his book.

"My job as a performer is to make sure that whatever happens in a performance lives in somebody else, that it's memorable."

— Yo-Yo Ma

4. ATHLETES & COMPETITORS

In Ancient Greece, the 'gymnasium' was a rehearsal space shared by orators and athletes. It was accepted that performances for both groups called for physical practice, the learning of technique and rehearsal. For both, this rehearsal included finding the mindset to be at your best, be it to step on the podium to speak in the forum or to line up at the start of a running race in the stadium.

A key difference was that the sporting win is an absolute. You win. Or not. The result is not dependent on artistic judgement or audience approval. The winning margin maybe a thousandth of a second, or a centimetre. And in some branches of professional sport, the win may be worth millions. It's no surprise many of the practice and rehearsal concepts that lead to results on the track or pitch are increasingly to be found in the dog-eat-dog world of business.

THE OLYMPIC GOLD MEDALLIST

I first met David Hemery on an athletics track. At that time, he, like me, was a 110 metre high hurdler. He had not then declared his ambition to specialise in the 400 metre hurdles, one of the most demanding of all track events. Certainly, too demanding and gruelling a training regime for me!

We met in serious competition once, in the 1966 Commonwealth Games held in Jamaica. In a close race, he won the Gold, I had to make do with Silver. His already formidable approach to training, leaving nothing to chance, gave him the edge as he drew past my tiring self, to win. Put simply, he was the fitter!

For him the high hurdles, valuable in mastering the hurdling technique, were a stepping stone in his quest for world class in the longer race. For this he not only trained and practiced harder than most. He rehearsed in his mind.

In today's professional sport, visualisation is not unusual. David, competing in the days when Olympic athletes were strictly amateur, was an early exponent. To race successfully, to manage himself, his rivals and the ten barriers, it was no good starting flat out and hoping others would fade. All had achieved similar times. He needed to execute his performance to optimise his own energy, and to out-think his rivals.

He spent time rehearsing in his mind all the possible situations he might face in the race. What if there is a strong tail or headwind? What if it's wet? What if it's very hot? What if someone races ahead, could he trust his pace judgement? He visualised racing in every single possible lane draw. He mentally raced every feared competitor, one-on-one, until he believed that if he ran to his potential, he could win. Having visualised and rehearsed every eventuality, he was ready, body and mind!

He was ready during the warm-up for his Olympic final. He tells this remarkable story of how he was seated, tying his shoes, when he caught sight of one of the favourites racing over the first three hurdles.

> "It appeared that he flew! So fast that my heart hit my throat! My reaction was totally counter-productive – I have to run faster than that!? I had to bring myself back into the most positive mental state in order to do my best. To do this, I took myself back mentally and physically to a time and a place when I was running very fast, gliding, in a state of mind of being in control, within the joyful feeling of powerful, fluid movement. It took less than two minutes, but the transformation of feeling and mental state was total: from weak to strong, from tense to relaxed, from anxious to confident."

I was in the stands and watched, in awe and amazement as David won in Mexico. One of the greatest Olympic performances ever, in one of the toughest events and he made it look effortless! It was a rare *sprezzatura* performance.

Sprezzatura, a word coined by 16th century Italian philosopher Baldassare Castiglione, has been variously described as the vital spark, the art of nonchalance, rehearsed spontaneity, practiced naturalness, joy in improvisation, embracing the unknown and enjoying it. That was David in that moment. However, he said that he didn't see that from inside. It was utter focus on pace judgement, effort distribution and will power; aiming to execute what he had mentally rehearsed hundreds of times.

After his hurdling days came to an end, David devoted much of his time to finding and encouraging young champions. He emphasised the mental approach that had worked so well for him, stressing the vital importance of increasing self-awareness and self-responsibility, essential characteristics of any successful performance.

"Reflecting on my experience in Mexico, I realised that I had aligned my body, mind, emotion and spirit in my quest to get the best from myself in that Olympic Games."

THE HALF-TIME TEAM TALK

"It was the most feared half-time weapon in football – and Sir Alex Ferguson's players all dreaded being on the receiving end of it. Fergie's 'hurled hairdryer' was a legendary force of discipline at Man United, and few were spared his wrath."

His was a unique approach to persuasive communication, but the half-time team talk is a staple of any manager's armoury. How do you raise the morale of a group of individuals who are losing badly, or change their defeatist mindset, or accept direction, or warn against complacency? And do this in a few minutes.

How do you prepare what to say, when late goals may have changed the game from a winning to a losing one, and the team from feelings of elation to despondency, just before the break. How do you rehearse to perform at your best, knowing your performance can turn the team from a losing to a winning one?

The talk may be in a sweaty dressing room, but it calls for the rhetorical concept of *kairos*. It is the timeliness of a talk, suited to the moment of speaking, fitting in words, and body language, to the mood and expectation of the audience. The experienced manager may not know *kairos* as a term, but he understands it.

Considered preparation and rehearsal is not possible in the time it takes to hurry from the dugout to reach the dressing room. Instead, the manager will be drawing on his experience of hundreds of other half-time team talks, learning from each. Every talk in effect is a rehearsal for the next one. Experience and instinct channel use of the three 'weapons' of communication when it matters. (As we saw earlier, Queen Elizabeth used them to great effect!)

Aristotle defined them as *ethos*, the appeal from the character, *logos*, the appeal to reason and *pathos*, the appeal to emotion. The manager seeking a change of tactics will call on *logos*, giving clear reason for the change. If a fighting spirit is needed, then *pathos*, emotion takes over.

However, these appeals count for little compared with *ethos*, the appeal of the character. It is the force of a personality and the trust of the players that creates truly powerful communication. Pep Guardiola, arguably the best manager in England, is captured in a leaked video that's gone viral. It shows a critical half-time talk and the team are losing. He says a few words, not easily heard. He actually speaks with his body. He puts himself on the line, every movement, every gesture, an outpouring of passion that is mesmerising, irresistible. The team won.

Another legendary coach, from the eighties, was Brian Clough, a larger-than-life character who broke the mould of the dour 'cloth cap' managers of the time. He was a brilliant, often outrageous communicator. He brought a touch of theatre and a few words to the shortest and, possibly, best team talk ever. His team, Nottingham Forest was playing badly and losing 2-0 at home. At half time, the players waited nervously in the locker room. They waited and waited and, moments before they had to go on for the second half, Brian Clough appeared and said:

"Sorry boys, my fault, picked the wrong team".

The 'wrong' team won.

THE TENNIS LEGEND

I watched on television the 2023 French Open final between Novak Djokovic and the ridiculously talented young Carlos Alcaraz. I wondered if his sublime talent would be enough to overcome the aura of invincibility, the mental preparedness of the much more experienced player. It wasn't. Novak won his 24th Open title, more than any other player. In an interview after the match, he said:

> "So, I leave those kinds of discussions, of who is the greatest to someone else. For me, on a daily basis, I'm the best on court, because with this state of mind, it's the only state of mind or spirit that can lead to historical results and this trophy. I'm writing my own history."

I'M WRITING MY OWN HISTORY.

In a separate interview his coach, Gorran Ivanisevic, talked about this 'state of mind' and the relentless approach to perfection, physical and mental.

"He did not come to this tournament with unbelievable confidence and form. I was not worried. I do not count these tournaments, Monte Carlo, Rome, anything. Only tournament counts is this one. Here he has this software in his head that he can switch on when a grand slam come. Grand slam is a different sport comparing other tournaments. He switches software. The day we arrive here, he was more motivated, he was more hungry, and every day he play better and better."

On working with him,

"Do you know I don't know what to do with him, it's always something, he wakes up and says my backhand is not working, we will work on his backhand, his backhand was already perfect for us, and then the service is not enough, everyday there is something, you know there is this genius mind, he's a perfectionist, there's always something missing ... everyday there's something, the stress level is always high, it never goes down, every day you will learn something, every day brings something new. And then he comes on court, you see how much he enjoys to practice, how much he enjoys to play, how much he enjoys the little details, to work on the little details."

In less colourful terms, Simon Briggs writing in the Daily Telegraph, suggested his mind-boggling achievements came "through analysing his own weaknesses and continuously evolving his game. In fact, his approach to tennis sounds like the classic scientific method – observation, question, hypothesis, experiment and conclusion."

GOOOOOO—OOOOL!!!

THE SPORTS COMMENTATOR

This celebratory yell has been called the Siren Song of football, the world's most popular sport. It originated in the early days of radio broadcast in Brazil. There, it was known as '*pelegrin de gol,*' meaning 'danger of a goal.' A warning call to listeners who may have strayed from the set. Today on television, goals around the world share the unmissable celebration. Apart from Britain – is this our so-called reserve, not so evident on the terraces?

An article in the New York Times captured its essence. "The cry of "goooool" is the exclamation point that captures a story's heart-pumping passage, the announcer's voice rising and falling harmoniously, and continuously whenever any team scores. If turned into a drawing, it would look like an arch. If it were a person, it would be the biggest guy in the room."

It takes skill and lungs. To succeed, soccer broadcasters must know how to scream their own version of the long drawn-out 'gooool', often for over 30 seconds. Some practice, in much the same way that opera singers do, rehearsing before they go on stage. One famous Brazilian broadcaster compared the cry to a tenor's high C and said, "there's a big dose of artistry involved." Another claimed, "It's your crowning achievement, or your moment of defeat."

There may be no 'siren song,' but each different sport will demand of their broadcaster passion and deep understanding. In the early days of live television, when a few channels held a monopoly of viewers, Dan Maskell ("Oh I say!") was known as the 'voice of tennis', Sid Waddell for bringing darts to middle England ("They've got Shakespeare on Radio 2, but you can't beat this!"). All knew David Colman, as the voice of BBC sport, enjoying the occasional hyperbole. ("Mike Parker, the veteran, evergreen, Peter Pan of British athletics!"– I was 28).

In today's multi-channel, multi-platform world, it is harder to stand out, but the good broadcaster can still be 'the voice' to many. To achieve this, their own authentic voice, they need to train and prepare, in much the same way as the athletes they are commenting on.

One such athlete is Stuart Storey, a rival from our high hurdling days. After competing at the Mexico Olympics, he went on to become the voice of BBC Television athletics, learning his craft covering ten Olympics. I asked him about his advice for would-be commentators:

"On preparation, you can cut no corners. For example, you need to know all there is to know about each athlete on the starting line, (you will have less than eight seconds talk for each as they wait for the starter's pistol). The commentator must decide which of the huge amount of information provided by the statisticians is relevant to each round of each event in a major Championship in particular."

"In team sports the commentator should learn all available data on the players of each team, as well as the substitutes who may come on to play a vital tactical role, even scoring a last-minute goal."

EXPECT THE UNEXPECTED.

"Expect the unexpected. It's what makes sport compelling, and it is what challenges the spontaneity of live commentary. It carries over to the venue. Be ready to 'fill in' when the lighting fails or the television picture, all of a sudden in the commentary position, is no longer available. Knowing how to switch from television commentary to radio is important, as they are different skills. From letting the picture tell the story, to describing every detail to create a picture in the mind of the listener is an art form."

For the live commentator, Stuart Storey's overarching advice is this:

"Say what the picture does not say and do this with a few well-chosen words. And, when you talk, use voice intonation and intensity, along with pace of delivery, to create atmosphere. The voice alone can let the viewer know how important a particular moment is."

His final advice is the dramatic use of …

Silence.

Know when to pause ... to let the action do the talking.

In an interview in the Guardian, Laura Woods, one of the only women who covered the 2022 World Cup, said broadcasting might look simple but it's not. "It's 'brutally' competitive." She started out by making YouTube videos in her garage, 'such brilliant practice ... and confidence comes with practice, it really does.' Her final words in the interview were eloquent and perceptive.

> "The one thing I learned is that a listener or a viewer can all smell any inauthenticity, and I figured that out really quickly. It wasn't that I wasn't trying to be me; it was that I was struggling with the confidence bit. But I kept doing it over, and over again and I got much more comfortable in my own skin.
>
> And that is the only thing you have got that no one else has, your own personality, your own way of doing things. It sounds like a cliche – just be yourself – but you really have to do that."

She was not, however, called on to cry "Gooooooooool!

THE HIGH HURDLER (MY STORY)

I have a temperature and my brow is hot. A bossy school matron orders me to the sick room. It's the day before our annual sports day and, as she takes my temperature, I ask if I'll be well enough to take part. Shaking the thermometer vigorously, she says, "we'll see how you are in the morning."

That night, I'm feverish and sleep fitfully, dreaming, perhaps hallucinating. In my dream, I'm at the start line for the hurdles. I've never hurdled before, tomorrow will be the first time. In my dream, with total clarity, I see myself on the starting line with the other boys. The sports master claps his hands. Without faltering, I run towards the first hurdle. I clear it without hesitation. No stuttering like the others. I sail over the hurdle. I know exactly how to fly over the next. I see each hurdle clearly in my dream. I repeat my effortless clearance each time. I win by the proverbial mile.

The next day my fever has gone. I'm ok to race. I line up for my first ever hurdle race. I hurdle literally as I dreamed. I win by the proverbial mile.

Looking back, I realise that I was engaged in visualising, rehearsing in the mind. I did not then understand this. Even though that dream was the start of what became a hurdling career that took me to two Olympics.

The dream left me with an inbuilt sense of timing that stayed with me as a hurdler. I still had to learn and practice, over and over and over again to master the difficult hurdling technique. And when I started to compete seriously, I did not hallucinate, but I did consciously apply the same visualising first experienced in my twelve-year-old dream.

In hurdles the start is everything. If you don't get to the first hurdle first, your race is as good as over. In the warm-up, I would 'see' the start, feel myself settling into the starting blocks, 'sense' the reaction to the gun. I approached the start itself with a sense of near euphoria, relishing the 'moment of truth'.

Through my time as a hurdler, all my hard work in practice, visualising the starts, were fuelled by a competitive nature. I wanted to be better. I wanted to win. That same nature carried through into my business career. Pitching for business, coaching others how to perform when it matters. Annoyingly, for those around me, I'm still rehearsing.

THE GREATEST OF ALL TIME. G.O.A.T.

I had my first, and only, boxing fight aged five. It was compulsory at my school. It would 'make a man of me.' I cried as I reluctantly climbed into the ring. Still crying, I held my arm out to keep the other boy away and cried, as I lost.

Since then, boxing has not been a sport I watched until the arrival of Muhammad Ali. At 18, he won Olympic Gold and went on to become the greatest boxer of all time. Arguably the greatest champion in any sport.

Physically superb, like a dancer in the ring, known for his 'Ali shuffle', he trained and practiced his craft as hard as anyone, "*I run on the road long before I dance under the lights.*" He was seen as an early pioneer of rap, winning two sounds 'Grammies.'

From the start, it was his mindset, his own unique mental rehearsal that set him apart. It was evident in the way he talked himself up.

"I am the greatest, I said that even before I knew I was."

It was evident in the way he won the most memorable fight in history, the *Rumble in the Jungle*, held in Kinshasha, Zaire in 1974. After three years of retirement, he was a 40:1 outsider against the invincible George Foreman.

And for eight rounds he risked destruction, allowing himself to be pummelled by sledgehammer blows. By then Foreman had punched himself out, drained of strength and of self-belief. Ali had seen this coming. He seized the moment, a moment he had somehow visualised through the pain, and struck, to knock him out.

Even before the fight, his mind, evidently, was at work. Foreman can't have enjoyed listening to this at the press conference:

"I've done something new for this fight. I done wrestled with an alligator, I done tussled with a whale; handcuffed lightning, thrown thunder in jail; only last week, I murdered a rock, injured a stone, hospitalised a brick; I'm so mean I make medicine sick."

GREAT MINDS

Gabby Thomas, one of the quickest women in history, has a degree in neurobiology from Harvard. She won 200 metre gold in the Paris Olympics. Shortly before her race, she was interviewed for the Guardian by Sean Inglis.

"Visualisation is huge for me. Part of my warm-up routine in every race is just visualising success. But I also do it the night before. I'm seeing everything. I am imagining who is lined up against me, everything from start to finish, and even how I'm going to celebrate at the end. Essentially, if you think about it enough and the mind starts believing it's true, then the body does as well. The mind is really powerful. It's insane how you can trick your brain into doing things and how your body follows."

"All things are ready if our minds be so."

—William Shakespeare.

5. TEACHERS & PREACHERS

Throughout history, preaching and teaching have been our most widespread, and frequently used means of formal communication. While the words can be interchangeable, preaching primarily has the aim of guiding or encouraging listeners to a particular belief, while teaching aims to educate, imparting knowledge. Both call for performance, with teaching usually more interactive whereas preaching is one way. The preacher tends not to seek debate. In fact, when coaching presenters, I find that "preaching" to your audience, and not listening is a common fault.

Preachers in most countries, and most faiths, deliver their sermons in often splendid churches and temples, the raised pulpits designed to elevate authority. Classrooms are more informal, the teacher needing to work harder to own the stage. A side note, in UK there are more pubs than churches. On average, each of the 20,000 vicars needs to conduct service at two churches. There are over 630,000 teachers working, performing in over 30,000 schools. A whole lot of performing going on!

PREPPING FOR THE CLASSROOM

Teachers will tell you they 'prep' for a class. I took this to mean brushing up on the subject, geography say, before the lesson started. I was wrong. In fact, they go through intense and focused rehearsal, probably more than any other profession. In my pitch coaching work, I soon realised my knowledge counted for little if I did not engage my audience. To do this, I had to perform, which called for rehearsal.

An excellent article by Noha Fikri of Toronto University, discusses *Teaching as Performance.* "Teaching is all about performance … it takes passion, and performance skills. Teaching is a cultivated practice that depends on much more than a well-prepared syllabus or a strong command of the content. Teaching is a full-bodied experience, one which requires an active engagement with every muscle of your body, along with full and undivided attention through which a teacher plays with and builds on student engagements to inform class content and discussions."

"The class is a stage, one in which the teacher's challenge is to keep the audience engaged and to hold their attention fully. Indeed, teaching is an entertainment business and what we do is perform in class."

THE CLASS IS A STAGE.

I discussed teaching as performance, and her approach to rehearsal, with geography teacher Sophie. She has been a teacher for only three years, but in that time she has been 'on stage' and delivered nearly three thousand performances! Four or five classes a day, each one lasting an hour and a quarter, each one to a different audience, whose make up and mood will vary by time and day of week. (Note, the *Guinness Book of Records* nominated David Raven who played Major Metcalfe, 'the most durable actor', for his 5475 performances in the still running *Mouse Trap*. Sophie will surpass that in two years!)

The parallel is not exact of course but, like an actor, she must prepare and rehearse to be at her best for each audience, each class. Often, she will only have fifteen minutes between lessons, sometimes less, to prepare.

"So, time of day has massive impact, say it is after break time, after lunch. Day of the week – Monday is completely different to Thursday or Friday. Different groups, high ability, low ability group. It might be they had an awards assembly in the morning, and that sets them off to come ten minutes late to lessons, suddenly they're all excited because they've been given sweets or chocolate, whatever it might be."

"So, for my first few years I used to rehearse by writing scripts, I literally wrote on pieces of paper shorthand, just as a prompt in case I needed it whereas now I just go for it and the way I plan is completely different to what I used to do."

"What I've learned to do is over-plan, you go in with the ideal plan, but I've three or four different avenues and plans that we can go along depending on how they react to the lesson. One thing I have learnt is sometimes things don't go to plan but that's ok because if you've got to adapt to what they are doing, and if you push through it's a better lesson, if you feel it's not working divert, it comes with confidence."

2000 years ago, Aristotle, who counted Alexander the Great among his students, identified the three appeals, covered earlier, that are the heart of persuasive speaking. They are worth repeating. *Logos*, the appeal based on rational argument, *pathos*, the appeal to the emotions and, too often overlooked, *ethos* the appeal from the character of the speaker. It was clear that Sophie employed all three to good effect with her students. An interesting demonstration of her 'character appeal' in action is the threshold concept.

"When a class starts and finishes, it's called the 'threshold' so I will always stand at the door, and I will say "good morning" to every one of the students that walks in. And as they leave, I'll say "have a good day". I'll have conversations with them, they may only be 3 seconds time, as they walk through. Some might guess what I'm going to say, "your shirt's not tucked in" or "you're looking happy today" – yes, I've won an award, or "that's a grumpy face, that's not like you," and they'll tell me something it's good for me to know. They may say they didn't get any sleep because a baby sister was crying all night, so I'll know what to expect. You get a gist of what you're going to be faced with."

Getting this 'gist' is akin to an actor or presenter reading the room, key to any performance. And like other performers, each lesson is a rehearsal for the next one.

I was struck by Sophie's search for and practice of 'hundreds of little strategies', like cold calling, how to ask questions to someone who knows the answer, the unconscious things like seeing someone fidgeting in the background or talking to a friend.

"I won't draw attention to it, I walk over and stand next to them, then they'll stop talking, but you don't want to draw attention to them. You are using body language a lot, massively. And, you've got the look, I'll stare, particularly at boys, it works massively, if they carry on talking, you just stare. It works really well; I enjoy doing it."

My final question for Sophie was this, "*Are you getting better as a teacher?*"

"Smarter! I am getting better at understanding how people learn. Sometimes I'll have five lessons with all the content the same, but the way I teach them is totally different. I'm lucky with my school. Of course, they set the agenda, but the how of teaching is very much down to me, the individual teacher."

FROM THE PULPIT

Like teachers, preachers are on stage regularly. Not the daily classroom, but for most, the weekly church on Sunday, needing a different sermon each week. Unlike teachers, whose audience is required by law to attend, congregations come of their own free will. In the case of the Church of England fewer and fewer are willing, the numbers have been falling for decades.

About thirty years ago, when working at Saatchi and Saatchi, (the agency had just successfully 'sold' Mrs Thatcher to the country so perhaps we could help sell God) I took part in a working meeting with senior C of E representatives. Its purpose was to identify ways of introducing a more promotional marketing approach. Might this offset the decline in church attendance? Could sermons be part of a more active approach?

The discussion was ended before it started when the scene was set for us with an explanation, almost an apology. "The Church of England was not an evangelical church that sets out to convert, but was one where the faithful found their own way in. What could be termed as powerful overt oratory was not expected of ministers."

To put it another way, Church of England vicars were not encouraged to fire up their congregations with the unbridled passion of the 17th cèntury evangelist John Wesley who said,

"Give me one hundred preachers who fear nothing but sin and desire nothing but God, and I care not whether they be clergymen or laymen, they alone will shake the gates of Hell and set up the kingdom of Heaven upon Earth."

Delivering stirring sermons but not 'shaking the gates of hell', in nearly empty church is a challenge. The group felt that in rising to the weekly task, vicars who were fully occupied on pastoral activity, spent more time crafting sermon content than on rehearsing its delivery. It was felt that some preachers having crafted the perfect sermon believed that the words alone (without emotional input from the speaker) would do the job. In effect, they were relegating themselves to the role of 'mouthpiece' as opposed to a passionate advocate.

They felt rehearsal, especially to an objective outsider, was not a regular practice. Lack of rehearsal can lead to the error of thinking more about yourself than about your audience. For the preacher, rehearsal reminds him to think about his audience and, of course, about God.

MARTIN LUTHER KING JR

A very different preacher, from a very different tradition – that of the Southern Baptist church in USA – was Martin Luther King Jr. His fervour was not inhibited. While his unforgettable 'Dream Speech', in front of the Lincoln Memorial in 1963, is seen as one of the defining speeches of the twentieth century, it was a sermon. King always described himself as a preacher.

He had delivered some 2,500 sermons in his lifetime, spending countless hours in preparation. He wrote them, memorised them, rehearsed them, and recorded them. The 'sound' of his voice, the poetic cadences, were critical. Once in the pulpit he never referred to his written text. He mastered the art of spontaneous performance, responding to the mood of his audience, to the emotion of the moment. Every sermon was a rehearsal for the next one.

For the very significant 'Dream Speech', he worked with colleagues to draft the text which was then handed out in advance to the media. It did not include the iconic "*I have a dream*" words. His impromptu departure from the prepared script at first glance seems an act of non-rehearsal. In fact, his certainty in reading the mood of his audience and the emotion of the moment was born from a life of rehearsal. This certainty allowed him to introduce and repeat the 'last minute' thought "*I have a dream*" eight times.

I HAVE A DREAM.

Some reports suggest he was prompted to use the words by gospel singer Mahalia Jackson, who shouted out, "tell them about the dream, Martin." King's own explanation is different …

"and all of a sudden, this thing came to me that I have used – I'd used it many times before, that thing about 'I have a dream' – and I just felt I wanted to use it here. I don't know why; I hadn't thought about it before the speech."

Perhaps the greatest rehearsed impromptu speech in history.

AI

The pandemic introduced widescale remote teaching and preaching. It was imperfect but served a purpose. Today the question is not when, but how will AI serve education and faith best. Are we handing over the most important of communication to an unconscious thing or can we harness the best of human and AI?

How might Aristotle have guided us? He might have advised leaving *logos*, the rational dissertation to the infinitely knowledgeable, but unfeeling AI teacher, to solve problems faster, find new solutions to time taking tasks.

Meanwhile, free up human everyday heroes to bring *ethos*, feeling and emotion, to lessons and sermons, with more time to rehearse, to empathise and engage with delivery that inspires.

"It's the teacher that makes the difference, not the classroom."

— Michael Morpurgo, Children's Laureate

6.

PERFORMANCE COACHES

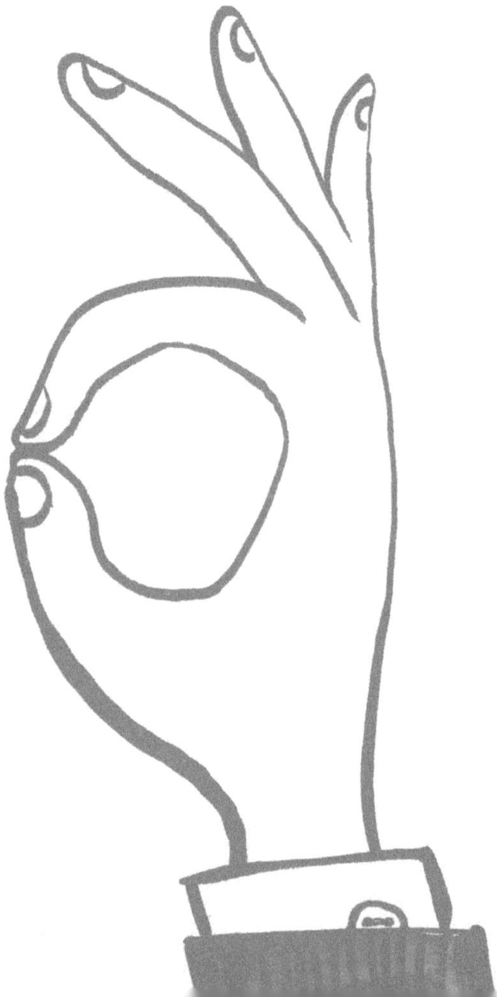

In my twenties, I was an accidental athlete with a degree of natural talent. I had ambitions to hurdle which would have come to nothing without my coach. He not only helped me develop the technical skill, overseeing my practice with an eagle eye for error, he guided me to discovering my best 'racing' self and to a mindset of competing with nerves but not fear, of relishing the moment.

In my late starting career as a pitch coach, I read widely, searched social media and devoured TED Talks. I was fortunate to come across four very different people each of whom influenced my communication, and of course my approach to rehearsal. Their expertise is wide ranging. Here, I've focussed on aspects that resonate with me – common sense, head space, voice and body!

COMMON SENSE MAKES SENSE

To many, Sir Anthony Jay is remembered as co-writer of the wonderful political satire, *Yes Minister*, first aired in the eighties. It was brought back as *Yes, Prime Minister*, still a regular on the rerun circuit.

A lesser number will know Jay as the founder, alongside John Cleese, of Video Arts in the seventies. He brought his considerable experience as a television writer and producer to the company, a pioneer of famously entertaining training programmes for business. To help his often inadequately prepared clients, he wrote a book of wisdom and commonsense, *Effective Communication*.

Whilst much of the book was written in the days before PowerPoint, the principles of good communication have never been better expressed. His thoughts on rehearsal never more valuable. To put these in context he prefaced his book:

"It is no more than a brief and very humble operating manual for those who, at some time or another, have to present ideas, decisions, facts or proposals to others in a context which demands something slightly more prepared and worked out than a chat over a drink, and who believe that it is worth spending some time and effort to achieve maximum clarity, conciseness, impact and persuasion: or at least to avoid alienation, catastrophe and humiliation."

He saw visual aids as a means not an end. At the time of writing, the commonly used aids were the flip chart, the overhead projector (OHP) and carousel driven slides. Remember them? Of the latter he said, "I can think of none that is used more ineptly than slides." I wonder what he might have said about (the curse of) digital slide technology.

To him, avoiding errors with visuals was what rehearsal was all about. The same errors are still common today. Errors like putting a slide on and taking it off without referring to it, standing between an audience member and the screen, constantly looking over your shoulder to see if the right slide has come up, talking to the screen not the audience, not removing a slide once there is no point to it.

Rehearsal he suggested, should also be used to check against the 'unnecessary slide', (less is more) the 'missing slide, the impact slide' (was it given its proper share of exposure) and he hated the purely verbal slide! "It's a killer, because words are what presenters are there for and what they are uniquely equipped to utter." He ends by saying "I honestly believe I have never seen a slide that had too little visual or verbal information on it."

On delivery, he is adamant that "you should not read a paper" (that anyone might have delivered in your place) and that "the best talkers are those who are the most natural, easy, fluent and free from the fetters that seem to bind others to small pieces of paper. They are talking only to us, and basing what they say to our reactions as they go along. Such a talk cannot, by definition, be scripted."

How do we achieve this? His answer lies in the difference between written and spoken English. If you write it out as written English and rehearse enough, you will have it by heart, but it will sound like a memorised document. If you start with spoken English, it will sound like an informal talk.

Professional broadcasters learn to write scripts in spoken English. For the amateur, a good way to 'translate' into spoken is to work on the script by rehearsing aloud, alone or to someone. Listen to your conversational self. "Are you using short words and short sentences?

Don't worry about grammar. Use your own words and phrases, the sort you actually use in conversation. Use active rather than passive verbs. Avoid anything that would sound oddly formal or stilted in normal conversation."

Rehearsing to someone is also the way to spot the common speaking errors:

"Mumbling, hesitancy, gabbling, catch phrases (the point is … sort of thing) poor-eye contact, mannerisms, dropping the voice." Rehearsal will also reveal what he saw as the chief problem to overcome, "speaker's rigidity." This stems from "using written English instead of spoken English and failure to realise that good speaking consists of addressing a large number of people as if they were a single person."

He ends with a 'thought-starter';

"Do the presenters you most enjoy listening to work from scripts or notes, or do they just speak spontaneously?"

GETTING IN THE RIGHT HEADSPACE

Do you have an idea worth spreading? If so, giving a TED Talk is your best opportunity. Performances are streamed live to over 100 countries. Your content will be vetted months in advance, you will be expected to talk without notes, with a minimal use of visuals and to keep to the allocated time limit, at most the now famous 18 minutes. Talking under pressure! So, if your idea is worth spreading, it is certainly worth rehearsing. Most speakers will spend countless hours in the run up, drafting and redrafting their script, rehearsing alone, to others, recording themselves.

One of the most celebrated talks was given by Susan Cain on the *Power of the Introvert.* In it, she talked about:

"My lifelong fear of public speaking, and about how I'd spent a year training in the style of a marathon runner to be the best and bravest speaker I could … The week before the conference, I cancelled everything on my calendar other than bath time with my kids. … I hired an acting coach, Jim, and rehearsed all day, every day, Monday through Saturday." Her talk has been viewed by over 30 million people.

Peter Botting is one of the UK's most experienced speaker coaches. I met him ten years ago when he lent his formidable communication skill to resolving a tricky political statement. He has rehearsed TED/ TED MED talkers for nearly ten years. He steps in when the pressure is building in the last few days before they go on stage. By this time their script has been vetted, the content cleared. His task is to help them to handle nerves and bring their best selves to perform when it matters most. Here's how he does this, in his own words:

Headspace.

Getting the speakers in the right head space is a big deal. Wimbledon winner Pat Cash's tennis coach, Ian Barclay, coached me as a tennis coach many years ago. He told me that coaching beginners is 95% technique and 5% head, but the ratio tilts as they become more accomplished and by the time they get to Wimbledon, it is over 95% head. My job is to get their heads in the right place, push their delivery and their body language from good to great and send them out "in the zone", and kicking.

You Need to Put the Work In.

There is no shortcut to being ready for the red dot*. There is no silver bullet. Giving a good talk means putting in a lot of time and effort. You can't outsource or delegate this. You are alone on the stage when you speak in public, and your performance will be related to the work you put into it. (*The red dot does more than symbolize TED Talks, it constrains the amount of space you can move in, on stage.)

Basic principles.

No selling; the telling of vivid and memorable stories – often personal ones; speakers speak without notes; the VERY limited use of PowerPoint and, when used, not the dull slides of the corporate world; self-effacing humour is welcomed and potent; being human and likeable is key to successful talks.

Less Is More.

A talk is not a thesis. You are not there to download all you know. You can say a lot in a very limited period if you work on your content. Easily digestible and accessible talks are best – this means being brief, focusing on a core message and delivering it really well.

A TALK IS NOT A THESIS.

Stories Sell.

Personal stories have an impact. They stir up emotion – but they should not necessarily be 'emotional'. Storytelling helps make your message sticky and accessible to audiences anywhere in the world.

Talk, Don't Act.

It's your voice that does the talking. It's a talk delivered on a stage – not a play. Staying within the famous red dot is important – moving about distracts from your message. Your words, your story and your delivery should be able to do everything required.

Take The Coaching.

Even the most experienced speaker can learn from a speaker coach ... Even a 5% improvement is noticeable – and everybody can improve with coaching. In a very short period of time, you have to help them do one or more (or all) of the following:

“Optimise their timing; put some magic in their introduction; focus them on the key messages and lines; calm and bolster their nerves or get their heads in the right place.”

FIND YOUR VOICE

I borrowed one of the best lines in my first book from Caroline Goyder. *"Pitches happen in the pauses."* I explained that practicing the pause, as if for thought, or emphasis, on reflection or to dramatize is an excellent way of creating interest, engaging your audience and managing your voice. I later shared a conference platform with Caroline where it was very clear she was the communications master, the consummate professional, I was the novice. I learnt a lot from her.

Caroline trained as an actor and went on to train actors as a voice coach at the Central School of Speech and Drama. She has since helped and inspired millions to use their voices well.

Her TED Talk, *The Surprising Secret to Speaking With Confidence*, has been viewed by over ten million people. As you might expect she speaks beautifully, with pauses of course, and her 'manly' wooden chest of drawers is one of best uses of a visual aid in any TED Talk. She recently published her third book, the remarkable *Find Your Voice*. Her talk and her book are 'musts' for anyone who wants to understand and learn how to improve and get the most out of their voice.

Here are a few of her many wise words. On the power of your voice:

"It's the infinite variety of your voice, its empathy, emotion, and nuance, that gives you the ability to influence. This is a different kind of soft power, and it matters."

On the need for practice:

"If you can chat with confidence to your friends, you can speak with confidence to a thousand people. If you can speak calmly and confidently in front of one audience, you can do it anywhere. You're using the same instrument. The question is how you access confidence under pressure. And the key to that confidence is in awareness and then practice."

And on rehearsing in the all-important moments before you step on stage:

"Once you have crafted your content, you have to rehearse. Thinking about the words isn't enough. Rehearsing in your head isn't enough."

"Until you've said the words out loud a few times to yourself, and ideally to someone else, you've really just written an essay."

"Speaking is physical. You have to get the words in the muscle. Rehearsal creates memory in the body that allows you to be instinctive and playful in front of an audience rather than having to overthink every word."

SPEAKING IS PHYSICAL.

“Think about anything physical that you’ve learned to do, from driving to dancing. You’ve learned it through rehearsal, practice and repetition. Lay down new habits so you can then get them in the muscle and be instinctive in the moment. The cost of not rehearsing is that the audience have to watch you working it out in front of them. Warming up in front of an audience this way is a cardinal sin of performers. The first few minutes are vital to the impression you make as a speaker. It’s painful to watch someone slowly getting up to full speed about five minutes in. So, take control.”

“Book sacrosanct time in your diary before a meeting or speech to think, prepare and rehearse. If you have said the words aloud before you speak them to the audience you will feel calmer, readier and your system will feel safer because you have a back-up drive in your brain. It can be far easier than you realise to rehearse, it’s simply a matter of speaking the words aloud a few times before you say them to the audience. You can do the first few run-throughs sitting on the sofa or in the garden. Then you will benefit from one or two rehearsals in front of a camera or person you trust.”

“Practise until you know your beginning, your signposts, and your ending, so you have at your fingertips the key points through the journey of your message. Then you can use them to orient yourself at any time when you need them as you will know how to get from one signpost to the next. This gives you ownership of your words and that easy conversational confidence."

"You don't have to memorise your speech word for word. When you have done enough work, you will know. When you are clear on your message you speak up with ease and openness, trusting yourself to read the room. Then you really stand out."

And just in case Caroline's belief in the vital role practice and rehearsal has escaped you, here are a few final words:

"I prepare to make sure I'm as ready as I can be. The safety net matters. To know I'm so prepped that it will be fine, no matter what."

OUR BODIES CAN CHANGE OUR MINDS

My career as a pitch coach started in 2010 in the years BC, Before Cuddy. I had experience from working on, and leading, a thousand advertising pitches. I was good strategically and technically. I was highly competitive and felt I had all the answers to coaching a pitch-winning team. How wrong I was. My innate shyness meant my own presenting style was forced and lacked ease or confidence when what the teams I coached needed, more than anything else, was a boost to their own confidence. Pitching can be a nerve-racking business and I was not delivering.

My career-saving epiphany moment was watching Amy Cuddy telling me how to *'fake it till you make it, and then fake it till you become it.'* Her now legendary TED Talk in 2012 has been viewed by over seventy million people and countless numbers of them will, like me, have found her words life-changing. The words and the way she said them, that is. Amy is mesmeric and irresistible in the way she brings her thinking alive.

FAKE IT TILL YOU MAKE IT.

A few days after viewing, I was able to put this to the test with my first ever live radio discussion, a national programme on the BBC. It was an important opportunity for me so, on arriving early in the morning at the BBC HQ off Regent Street, I spent ten minutes marching briskly round the building, stopping to do my Wonder Woman power poses, holding my arms aloft, looking somewhat deranged. However, I felt amazing. I surged into the studio, and I'm told, 'killed' my interview.

Her central premise is that while we know "our nonverbals govern how other people think and feel about us, we don't recognise that our nonverbals also govern how we think and feel about ourselves." Our body can change our mind. By adopting open expansive postures and power posing for a couple of minutes we will feel more powerful. Our testosterone, the dominant hormone, level goes up as our cortisol, the stress hormone goes down.

As we feel more powerful, we become more fully present, "confident, comfortable, and passionately enthusiastic." This is explored further in her wonderful book, *Presence*. Research shows how these characteristics are the most decisive factors in determining success in the job interview or competitive presentation. Regular practice, 'tiny tweaks' in everyday life situations will lead to big changes … till you become it.

Amy helped me lift morale when coaching final rehearsals and send people confidently and optimistically into the most challenging pitch or interview. I would demonstrate power posing, fists pumping the air, adding a power shout "I am the greatest," after all it worked for Mohammed Ali! I urged that they 'faked it' in the last minutes before going on stage. Even, or especially, the many who are reluctant about rehearsal, who say 'I'm not prepared, my script is not ready, I'm too busy,' meaning 'I'm nervous'. They will feel will the release of energy and confidence.

As Amy says

"At some point you must stop preparing content and start preparing mind-set. You have to shift from what you'll say to how you say it."

LUDUS MAGNUS

As long as mankind has been competitive, on track or stage, coaches have played their part. Never more so than with gladiators fighting in Roman arenas. In over 100 gladiator schools, trainers were called *Doctores*, each specialising in a specific combat form – *Secutorum* (slashers), *Laquerarii* (lasso), *Paegniarius* (whip, club and shield).

They subjected the *novicii* to gruelling training. The *tetrad*, a four-day cycle of combat drills, weightlifting, high intensity interval work, et al that would more than challenge today's elite athletes. Arguably, they pioneered understanding of the winning mindset, the right 'headspace'. Happily, the art of dying with grace and honour is no longer on the curriculum.

"They are able who think they are able."

— Virgil

7. CONCLUSION

I started this book with the words of poet Sean O'Casey, *"All the world's a stage and most of us are desperately unrehearsed."* The stories I've told are from people whose stages range from the pulpit to the classroom, the boardroom to the broadcast studio, the sports arena to the concert platform. Some are of extreme, almost brutal rehearsal, some are unexpected, others more expected but impressive.

They are not 'desperately unrehearsed', and I hope their stories will inspire those that are! And that's most of us much of the time.

Most of us can benefit from time spent rehearsing, readying ourselves for everyday moments in life, moments that matter, from making peace with our neighbour over the invasive fence, persuading a recalcitrant child, asking for the salary we know we deserve, preparing for dinner guests to talking ourselves out of something, or into it, to thinking before speaking, smiling when we don't feel like it, listening with empathy, being our best selves.

As Steve Jobs, whose rehearsed presentations persuaded us to keep thinking *Apple*, said:

"Be ready to catch the ball when it is thrown by life."

ENCORE

Here are some final words from William Shakespeare.

Hamlet's Advice to the Players:

"Speak the speech, I pray you, as I pronounced it to you, trippingly on the tongue: but if you mouth it, as many of your players do, I had as lief the town-crier spoke my lines. Nor do not saw the air too much with your hand, thus, but use all gently; for in the very torrent, tempest, and, as I may say, the whirlwind of passion, you must acquire and beget a temperance that may give it smoothness."....

.... *"Go make you ready."*

THE LEGENDS & EVERYDAY HEROES

These are the people whose stories, and wisdom, enabled me to write this book. Some of the stories are taken from history books, published articles and public broadcasts. Others came from live interview. My special thanks to all of those who gave me their time.

History makers: Demosthenes, Abraham Lincoln, Nelson Mandela, Queen Elizabeth I, Robert Ascham, Adolph Hitler, Winston Churchill, King George VI, Ronald Regan, Quintilian.

Business Leaders: Steve Jobs, Ciaran Bird, Clive Woodward, David Burke, Edward Gardener, Olga Turner, Duncan McLoud, Truman Capote, T.F. Freije, John Hays, Sun Tzu, Camine Gallo.

Stage Performers: Esther Abrami, Imogen Sage, Wincanton Choir, Katrine Reimers, Andre Constand, Adam Kay, Taylor Swift, Yo-Yo Ma.

Athletes & Competitors: David Hemery, Baldassare Castiglione, Alex Ferguson, Pep Guardiola, Brian Clough, Novak Djokovic, Gorran Ivanisevic, Simon Briggs, Stuart Storey, Laura Woods, Muhammad Ali, Gabby Thomas, William Shakespeare.

Teachers and Preachers: Noah Fikri, Sophie, John Wesley, Martin Luther King Jr, Aristotle.

Performance coaches: Anthony Jay, Peter Botting, Caroline Goyder, Amy Cuddy, Ludus Magnus doctores, Virgil.

My thanks also to these everyday heroes, soon to be legends, who helped me with this book:

Jennifer, my talented editor and designer. Christian who read, suggested and encouraged me throughout. Dom whose idea it was. And to Eliza, for ignoring my excuses of writer's block.

REHEARSAL PRACTICE

These stories aim to inspire rehearsal. For ideas on *how* to rehearse, my on-the-go guide, *Don't Risk It, Rehearse It!* gives practical advice. Designed for easy reading on a phone (see QR code below) or tablet, it is freely available and downloadable at

www.pitchwisdom.com/rehearse

Michael is also the author of

It's Not What You Say,
It's The Way You Say It!

and

Unaccustomed As I Am…
The Wedding Speech Made Easy.